The D

The Ultimate Really Really Bad Dad Joke Book

by

Gary Rowley

Images Created by Freepik

You've seen the rest, now meet the best: The Daddy, the ultimate in bad Dad joke books, penned with that oh-so special person in mind - your Dad!

Packed with 100s of terrible gags and truly awful puns, it's the joke book equivalent of taking a cat to a pigeon fair, a fatherly feast of mirth and merriment, ammunition aplenty to tease and torment as only a Dad can!

So go on, I dare you: treat the old man to a copy, then skedaddle to a dark room somewhere while he works his magic. As it says on the guarantee, he'll love it - you'll hate it!

Enjoy!

Dedicated to super funny Dads everywhere - salute!

CONTENTS:

Dedication Page:

To... Birth day boy

From... Oscar

Message... Happy 42nd
Birthday - may this book
keep you smiling, and
drive sophie crazy ! xx

Bad Dad Jokes: 1-150 – Truly Awful!

1. I've started work as a waiter. Granted, the money's not fantastic; but at least I can put food on the table...

2. My fear of horse chestnut trees. After years of therapy, I've finally managed to conker it.

3. So I said, doctor, doctor, every time I go for a number two, it comes out looking like chips. He said, have you tried pulling that string vest up a bit?

4. I bought a mobile phone off a vicar. It was a pray as you go.

5. My pet mouse, Elvis...he was caught in a trap.

6. I asked this bloke what his American Pit Bull puppies were going for. He said, anything they can get their teeth into...

7. Delivery driver walks into the medical centre and slams a dozen pizzas down on the counter. He says, before anyone asks, it's just what the doctor ordered.

8. This bloke emptied a packet of grated cheese over my head. I said, that was mature, wasn't it...?

9. I rang the gaffer. I said, I'm just arriving on the south coast now, boss. He said, do you realise it's five in the morning? And what are you doing on the south coast? I said, just what you said, boss: making sure I was in Brighton early.

10. I said, I can't believe how much weight I've put on. I might have one of those over active, erm, erm...She said, thyroid gland? I said, no, knife and fork!

11. I've finally fulfilled my lifetime's ambition and opened a second-hand fridge shop. Honestly, I'm absolutely buzzing...

12. I've been offered a job in a bubble-gum factory. I've told them I'd like to chew it over first.

13. It's just been on the news that United have signed Edward Scissorhands. By all accounts, he looked really sharp during his trial.

14. Every time the phone rings, it's someone telling me I've got a forest of big trees growing at the bottom of the garden. I'm sick of all these blooming oaks calls...

15. I'm writing a book about cricket defensive batting techniques. My friends say I need to get out more...

16. Finally retired after fifty years of toil in the washing line factory, the bloke next door's only gone and pegged it, hasn't he?

17. I hired a handyman who couldn't stop thinking he was a James Bond villain. I said, Doctor know? He said, it's Goldfinger, actually; now, these Odd Jobs...

18. East End mob rule: it was all the Krays.

19. I found a hedgehog in my pint. I thought, this has been spiked.

20. Youth goes on the Antiques Roadshow, showing off a rare Ming Dynasty vase. Presenter says, this is worth twenty thousand pounds. Can I ask where you got it from? Youth says, it was passed down to me, mate. Presenter says, passed down to you from where? Youth says, from this bedroom window…

21. I took my PC back to the shop when it wouldn't stop swearing at me. I said, I think it might be the curser…

22. I invested every penny I had in a second-hand Cessna then went into business, offering cut-price flights around town. Just my luck: it never really took off.

23. So I said, I'm off on a right do tonight: a fiver in and drink as much as you want. He said, where's that at, like? I said, the local swimming baths!

24. I said, doctor, doctor, I can't stop singing Gloria Gaynor songs. Quack said, I Will Survive? I said, I know you will, but it's me I'm worried about!

25. There's more to my trainee hangman's job than I thought. But not to worry: I'm sure I'll soon get the hang of it.

26. Is Brexit what happens when a fat bloke sits on a rickety chair...?

27. Golfing shoes for sale. Hole in one.

28. I went to see a band called the Dalmatians. Never again, I can tell you: they did 101 spots.

29. Cowboy goes to the vets. Receptionist says, Buffalo Bill? He says, no, actually; I've come to collect my pet cat.

30. I wasn't impressed with the fine print of my pension. Apparently my next of kin is some geezer called Benny Fishery.

31. I arrived home to find our kid asleep on a privet. He always did live life on the hedge.

32. Apparently Marvin Gaye's on at the Dog & Duck later. And, before you ask, I heard it through the grapevine...

33. I was invited to a party at the launderette and went home with a box of washing powder. I won it in a game of pass the Persil.

34. Did you hear about the fight in the vacuum cleaner factory? Apparently it was a right old dust up.

35. I lost a needle in a haystack. I found it in the end, like; but it was like looking for a needle in a haystack.

36. Did you see Rooney nearly score with a curler on the footie last night? It was still in his hair from the night before and the ball skimmed his bonce when he went up for a header.

37. I went to buy a new car with our kid. This salesman said: Gobble-gobble, gobble-gobble. And our kid replied: Gobble-gobble, gobble-gobble. I think they were talking turkey.

38. This bloke asked if he could give me a performance of his British bird song repertoire. I said, if you must; but I am in a hurry. Is it alright if we just whistle through it?

39. I went to the quacks, thinking I was a moth. Doctor said, it's not me you need: it's the psychiatrist next door. I said, I know that, like. It's just that, well...I saw your light on, didn't I?

40. I went for this interview at the supermarket: the manager warned it was hard graft and that I'd need to be driven. I said, if I could afford a chauffeur, mate, do you seriously think I'd need a job at the Co-op?

41. This bloke asked what I knew about elephant hides. I said, not much. In actual fact, it's a bit of a grey area.

42. I packed in my job at the bacon factory on medical grounds. I kept coming out in rashers.

43. My new 2000cc car scoffed my electric drill, lawnmower and spanner and screwdriver sets. I've only myself to blame: I should never have bought a tool-eater in the first place.

44. This bloke emptied a packet of grated cheese over my head. I said, that was mature, wasn't it...?

45. I was wrongly accused of stealing a crate of dilute orange. Fortunately, all charges were eventually quoshed.

46. Last night's documentary about North Sea oil exploration: *Bo-ring!*

47. Traffic News: The M1 remains closed tonight after a lorry spilled a load of snooker extensions across three lanes of busy motorway. Police have warned motorists to expect long cues.

48. I see that film's on again later, the one where occupants of an Antarctic research station discover an alien in a block of ice and then fight to stay alive as it consumes them one by one. Straight after that, it's the remake. Honestly, if it's not one Thing it's another.

49. A fight broke out at the Shakespearean night when a bloke in row three developed an annoying tickle. If you ask me, it was Much Ado About Coughing...

50. I went for an interview for this motorcycle stuntman's job, unaware that I was in competition with a couple of hundred others. Not that I let it get in my way: I jumped the queue.

51. My friend Harvey drinks vodka and orange juice by the gallon and makes a living from picture hanging. Just in case you wondered, his surname is Wallbanger.

52. I went on a weekend break to Berlin and fell out with everyone I met. I was obviously having a bad Herr day.

53. There was this brilliant programme on last night about how blue bottles use suction to adhere themselves to vertical surfaces. Honestly, it was the best fly on the wall documentary I've ever seen.

54. I went to the quacks, complaining of double vision. Doctor Hourihane and Doctor Hourihane couldn't have been more understanding.

55. First day at work, the gaffer told me to pop a roll of bubble wrap in the corner. I don't think he was best pleased when I was still popping it eight hours later...

56. I've applied for a historian's job but wish I hadn't bothered. I mean, where's the future in it?

57. Our kid's been driving round town all week, taking pictures of water-filled pot-holes. If you ask me, he's blinking puddled...

58. Patient: Doctor, doctor, I keep thinking I'm John McEnroe. Quack: You *cannot* be serious!

59. So I said, I've heard there's this nudist beach opened on the canal bank if you fancy taking a look? She said, I'd love to; but unfortunately I've got something on...

60. Did you hear about the shoplifter that was caught in possession of a boxful of topical acne cream? He was given an on the spot fine.

61. I took my car to the garage, complaining of hissing noises whenever it rained. The mechanic said it sounded like the windscreen vipers.

62. After yet another defeat, the manager of the Exorcist's football team blamed a lack of spirit in the dressing room...

63. I said, how's the new job at the cobblers? He said, haven't you heard? I got the boot!

64. This bloke offered to teach me how to do the Fosbury Flop. I jumped at the chance.

65. I've just seen a blacksmith having a fight with a hairdresser. They were going at it hammer and tong!

66. So I said to Steven Spielberg, which way is Panavision, mister? He said, never heard of it, pal. I said, you're such a liar: your last movie was filmed there!

67. I'm on a crash diet. Yup, I keep driving my car into brick-walls so that all my cash goes on repairs instead of burgers and fish and chips.

68. My daughter told me not to waste money buying her a bike for Christmas. She said she'd just found one round the back of the wardrobe.

69. I got a job as a human cannonball. Two hours later, I'd been fired...

70. What goes broom-broom, broom-broom? United's open-top bus, reversing into the garage for another year.

71. This landlord asked me if I wanted a chimney. He said, go on, treat yourself; it's on the house...

72. I was walking round B&Q when this bloke in an orange apron asked me if I wanted decking. Luckily for me, I managed to get in first...

73. Him: What's the most common owl in Great Britain? Her: Is it a barn owl? Him: Nope. Her: Tawny owl? Him: Nope. Her: What, then? Him: It's a tea towel, silly!

74. Traffic chaos ensued today when a lorry load of castanets collided with a lorry load of tambourines. Drivers of both vehicles were said to be badly shaken.

75. Life was going great until I opened that blooming ski slope. Unfortunately, it's been downhill ever since...

76. I failed to turn up for my interview at the fizzy pop factory. No real reason: I just bottled it.

77. I went on a visit to the local RSPCA office and couldn't believe how tiny it was. Honestly, there wasn't enough room to swing a cat.

78. My pal stuck his head in a bad tempered stallion's gob and it bit his nose clean off. Moral of the story: never look a miffed horse in the mouth.

79. I said, I'm a bit worried about our kid: he's totally obsessed with James Bond films starring Sean Connery. She said, Dr No? I said, not that I'm aware. Besides, it's not a doctor he needs, it's a flipping psychiatrist!

80. The missus went to a fancy dress party in a taser costume. I don't think I've ever seen her look so stunning.

81. I fell madly in love with a hide and seek champion. Not that it lasted, like; she soon found someone else.

82. What did Field Marshall Rommel say to his men just before they got in their tanks? Come on now, lads: get in them tanks!

83. I was driving home in my new car when I broke down. I thought, I'll never keep up the repayments...

84. There was this bloke at the gym, sparring with Hank Marvin. Ooh look, I thought: Shadow boxing.

85. I went to see a band called the Polos. They were absolutely mint.

86. It's just been on the news that the calendar factory is in financial trouble. It sounds to me like its days are numbered.

87. This bloke asked me if I'd ever seen the Abominable Snowman. I said, not Yeti...

88. I'm still not keen on my new television salesman's job. I'm finding it hard to switch off at night.

89. Noticing my reaction after walking past the mouth-watering aroma of the new Chinese restaurant, the wife decided to treat me. Yup, she walked me past again...

90. I went to see a comedian called Humpty Dumpty. Honestly, he was so off the wall.

91. Our kid reckons he's starting a balloon flights company. I'll believe it when I see it, like; if you ask me, he's full of hot air.

92. What do you call an American soul singer with a finger up his nose? Wilson Pick-it.

93. I've landed a job in an itching powder factory. Needs must, I suppose; at least I'm still scratching out a living.

94. When I won tickets to the British Soap Awards, the missus rented a Chas Dingle costume to celebrate. You should have seen the look on her face when Imperial Leather won first prize.

95. Bloke goes to the doctors, complaining he was six inches shorter than this time last week. Quack says, it's not me you need, matey...it's a blooming shrink!

96. I've resigned from my job at the KP factory: the pay was flipping peanuts.

97. The president of the UK Rocky Balboa Appreciation Society was visiting the big cat enclosure at Chester zoo, when a piece of sign fell off and knocked him unconscious. Investigations revealed it was the 'I' of the tiger.

98. So I said, I don't suppose you haven't phoned the Police have you? It's just that, well...there's Sting and Stewart Copeland at the back door.

99. Did you hear about the lumberjack who had his tools stolen? He took it extremely well by all accounts: he said he'd no axe to grind...

100. The wife didn't speak to me for a week on account of my obsession with Hollywood boxing films. It all blew over eventually, though; we were just going through a Rocky patch.

101. I went to the doctors, thinking I was an alarm clock. He told me not to worry, like; he said it was probably just a wake-up call...

102. There was this bloke in the pub, carrying five pints of beer, ten vodka and limes and sixteen packets of beef crisps. I said, do you want this tray, mate? He said, do I heckers like: I've got enough to carry!

103. I bumped into Billy the Kid on his way into the bank. I said, fancy a chinwag, Billy? He said, I'd love to; but unfortunately I've got to shoot...

104. I decided to have forty winks while the wife got ready to go and see her favourite Wham tribute band. I said, make sure you wake me up before you go-go...

105. That big trumpety thing grandad always used to help him understand what people were saying; he's only gone and dropped it, hasn't he? Even worse, it went straight beneath the wheels of a number 22 bus. Talk about the end of an hearer...

106. I was out with the wife when this bloke suddenly set fire to himself right in front of us. She said, take no notice; it's just an old flame...

107. I went in HMV and asked for Lou Rawls. Assistant said, loo rolls, sir? Have you tried the household goods shop next door...?

108. This psychiatrist said I didn't really exist then asked how I felt about it. I told him I was made up...

109. I went to the shop for a bottle of tomato sauce. Shopkeeper said, HP? I said, no, thanks; I'll be paying cash if it's all the same with you.

110. Our kid's attempt at breaking the world plate spinning record...he's only gone and smashed it!

111. I lied all the way through my interview for a job in the X-ray department at the hospital. I didn't get it, of course: they saw straight through me.

112. A friend of mine was annoying me with bird puns. I thought, toucan play at that game...

113. We ducked for cover on the 18th green when the shout went up: Fore! As my mate started to get up again, I said: Stay down: there's three more to come yet!

114. When I joined the army, I got into endless arguments on the parade ground. It was all the officers fault: it was them who kept telling everyone to fall out...

115. I've just been offered a job as a toilet salesman: thirty grand per year and choice of company carsie...

116. Bloke calls the surgery. He says, I can't stop thinking I'm a dog: can I make an appointment? Receptionist says: Of course; what name is it, please? He says, Jack Russell...

117. Getting baby to sleep: it's hardly rock-it science, is it?

118. I answered the door to a trio of Irish lumberjacks. Whey hey, I thought: tree fellers...

119. Could I heckers like remember where I'd left my boomerang: then it came back to me...

120. Deep sea diving, I got straight on the intercom when my leg was bitten off by a shark! This voice said: Which one? I said: How am I supposed to know? There's hundreds of them down here!

121. I bumped into this Arabian prince, singing Bill Haley and the Comets songs, while buying baby toys and eating a tuna and mayonnaise baguette. Talk about Sheikh, rattle and roll...

122. There were all these people, shoving each other about outside the school gates. Ooh look, I thought: pushy parents.

123. I went to the doctors, thinking I was a dog. Quack says, and how long have you felt this like this? I said, ever since I was a pup.

124. The wife made me promise not to forget to buy her something pearl for our 30th wedding anniversary and I was true to my word. I don't think she was best pleased, mind, when I turned up with a buy 2 get 1 free deal on 40w lightbulbs...

125. I didn't enter adulthood until my late teens. And now bad timekeeping has cost me my job at the photo lab. There's no denying it: I'm a late developer.

126. I was doing brilliant in the pub quiz until question 16: who had a hit with the very best of Status Quo? How was I supposed to know? I wasn't born until the year 2001!

127. The woman next door has resigned from her job on the maternity ward after forty years of service. I can only think she's going through some kind of midwife crisis.

128. I got a job as an undertaker then signed for the local football team. Ten minutes into my debut, this cross came in and guess what? Yup, I absolutely buried it...

129. When I was in the army, I led this patrol into no-man's-land to check-out a bacon tree. As soon as we got near, though, all hell broke loose. It turned out it wasn't a bacon tree, after all: it was a flipping ham bush...

130. I was offered my old job back, muck-spreading at the farm. I said, no, thanks; I like to think I've put it all that behind me...

131. How did Mary and Joseph know baby Jesus weighed 7lb 12oz? Because they had him a-weighed in a manger.

132. I went to the doctors. I said, every time I roll over in bed, I wake up in fits of laughter. He said, and how long have you been having these funny turns...?

133. Bad news, I'm afraid: a pile of Snoop Doggy Dog and Kanye West CDs went missing from the record shop where I work. Just so long as they don't think I'm taking the Rap for it.

134. I was only a day old when this kid in the next cot tried to sell me a dodgy rattle. I said, do you think I was born yesterday...?

135. Apparently Botham's Ashes is on later. I can't believe it: it was only the day before yesterday I was listening to him commentating on Test Match Special!

136. I received a letter from Sitting Bull's solicitor. I can't believe it, I thought: I'm being Siouxed!

137. I went to the shop for a packet of salt and vinegar crisps, but finished up splashing the cash on a Boeing 737. They only had plane...

138. I've got a tree in the back garden that keeps making doggy noises. I think it must be the bark.

139. Teacher: Can anyone define the word, geriatric? Boy: Is it three goals by a German footballer, Miss?

140. I took my pet frog to the library but wished I hadn't bothered. Every time I showed it a book, it went, reddit, reddit, reddit...

141. Mobile phones have been around longer than people think. I was watching this film the other night and distinctly heard Sir Lancelot ask someone to fetch his charger.

142. I was offered this job with a starting pay of £10 per hour, rising to £20 per hour after six months. I told them I'd start in six months!

143. All this talk about new plastic banknotes lasting longer than the old paper ones is complete and utter bunkum. A cup of tea and a slice of cake and it's gone, just the same...

144. I spotted this taxidermist, eyeing up my pet rabbit. I told him to get stuffed.

145. It was nearly dark when I arrived at art class and discovered Sir Lancelot, sketching a pub. It's right what they say, I thought: the blooming knights are drawing inn...

146. Tardis for sale. £100. No time wasters, please.

147. Did you hear about the extinct bird that started work at the bread shop? It kneaded the dough-dough.

148. I've got a joke about construction but I'll have to tell you it tomorrow. I'm still working on it...

149. After finishing university, I had my front teeth out then went back-packing around Europe. I was having a gap year.

150. I discovered I was dyslexic when I went to a toga party...dressed as a goat.

Bad Dad Jokes: 151-300 – Even Worse!!

151. So I said, with all that's going on in the world, do you think we should have the right to bear arms? She said, I thought we already had? I mean, no one's ever stopped me from wearing a T-shirt!

152. I'm writing a follow up to War and Peace but wish I'd never started. Honestly, it's like writing War and Peace...

153. Just think: if Whoopi Goldberg had married Peter cushion, she'd have been Whoopi Cushion...

154. I've written a play about coping with conjunctivitis in the mean streets of Manchester. It's a gritty northern drama...

155. We were drawn away in the cup against a team of builder's merchants, who insisted upon playing on a sand and gravel pitch. We lost 4-2...on aggregate.

156. I said, I got that job at U-Boat weekly. She said, sub editor? I said, what do you think?

157. This bloke tried selling me a mountain for £10,000. I told him it was a bit steep.

158. I said, doctor, doctor, I can't stop sighing with relief. He said, you're obviously a man of phew words...

159. Three sheets to the wind, I carefully removed my shoes, coat, trousers and pants then gently tiptoed upstairs. It was only when I reached the top that I realised I was on the number 22 bus home...

160. I'm not saying I'm hard up, like; but I've asked the woman next door if she'd mind sewing a shirt on my button for me.

161. I said to this architect, what are you doing this weekend? He said, for once in my life, I've no plans...

162. My acupuncturist job: I'd pack it all in for two pins.

163. I bought a job lot of hangman's nooses then doubled my money by selling them one at a time on EBay. Talk about money for old rope.

164. This bloke showed me his collection of 10,000 back copies of the Radio Times. I thought, he's definitely got a few issues...

165. I got that job at the cemetery, but I'm still not sure if it's full or part-time. I need to do a bit of digging...

166. Did you know that, by law, you have to turn your headlights on when it's raining in Sweden? Can someone please explain how the heck I'm supposed to know when it's raining in Sweden?

167. I was shocked to see this chocolate bar, rushing to the rescue of an old lady, surrounded by muggers. Whey hey, I thought: a have a go Aero...

168. I went to see this clairvoyant. A sign on the door said: Closed due to unforeseen circumstances.

169. Moving to Rome to take on a curator's job at the Colosseum was the biggest mistake I've ever made. My life: it's in ruins.

170. I asked my mate how his bouncer's course went. He said he'd fill me in later...

171. After a holiday from hell, I wrote a strongly worded letter to the travel company, then stuck the envelope in a vice and attacked it with a rasp. When the wife asked what I was doing, I said, what do you think? I'm filing a complaint!

172. I went to the chemist and that woman was in again, the one who used to work at McDonalds. I said, a box of laxatives, please. She said, to go? I said, what do you think...?

173. Ok, so I've no idea what apocalyptic means: it's not the end of the world, is it?

174. I asked this puppeteer if he could find me a job. He said, leave it with me: I'll see if I can pull a few strings.

175. That housewarming party I attended certainly lived up to its billing. The flipping kitchen caught fire...

176. I've moved into a flat above the hairdressers where I always used to go for my hair cutting. Yup, I've gone back to my roots.

177. Paddy, the electrician, refused to touch the malfunctioning electric chair at the prison where he worked. He said that, in his professional opinion, it was a flipping death trap.

178. I don't mind admitting it: my professional boxing career was a complete disaster. But at least no one can say I didn't take it on the chin.

179. That job at the chicken farm: apparently I'm well down the pecking order...

180. The wife's applied to become an air hostess. if you ask me, she's off her blooming trolley.

181. I've got an Irish spider. It's a paddy long legs.

182. This youth off our street was rushed to hospital after overdosing on curry powder. Last I heard, he'd slipped into a korma.

183. I went to the bank to arrange some finance. Assistant said, sorry, sir, but the loan arranger isn't in today. I said, how about Tonto...?

184. Teacher: Can anyone spell the word, farm? Pupil: Is it E-I-E-I-O, sir? Teacher: E-I-E-I-O? How do you make that out? Pupil: Old MacDonald had a farm, E-I-E-I-O.

185. I was up before the beak for possession of a live hand grenade. Much to everyone's relief, it was thrown out of court...

186. When I got this tip off, I got straight on the phone to the police. I don't think they weren't best pleased when they turned up and I showed them my broken snooker cue.

187. The bloke that invented mobile phone spell correctors died yesterday. May he restaurant in peace...

188. I bought the wife a DIY colonic irrigation kit for her birthday. She told me to stick it where the sun doesn't shine.

189. Unable to sleep since turning professional boxer, I finally went to the doctors. Quack said, have you tried counting sheep? I said, course I have; but every time I reach nine, I get up again!

190. After the election of Donald Trump, there's a new sign in our local library that says: Anyone seeking post-apocalyptic fiction, please now go to the current affairs section.

191. I booked in for cosmetic surgery and woke up with dozens of little furry bunnies, grafted into my scalp. I said, blimey O'Reilly: I've had a blinking hare transplant!

192. I went to bed Sunday night and woke next morning to find myself surrounded by dozens of cartoon bears, singing The Bare Necessities. It was a bad case of Monday morning Baloo's.

193. Last night's documentary about projectile vomiting: it brought it all back.

194. I went to the doctors, complaining of dizzy spells. Quack said, you're sure it's not all in your head, aren't you?

195. I phoned the pizza shop. I said, a large stuffed crust Hawaiian, please. Assistant said, do you want that cutting into eight or twelve pieces? I said, make it eight...I'd never eat twelve!

196. Muhammad Ali figurine for sale. £50 ono. Not boxed.

197. I was stuck on the motorway for hours by what was supposedly a shed load. Yeah, right; when I reached the scene, there wasn't a shed in sight: it was a consignment of blooming washing machines!

198. I bought a job lot of Treasure Island films then made a beeline for the car boot sale. Just my luck: all my stock was confiscated and I was charged with flogging Pirate DVD's.

199. People laughed when I told them I'd invented an invisibility cloak. If only they could see me now...

200. William Shakespeare walked into a pub. The landlord told him he was Bard...

201. I've enrolled for anger management classes. Apparently it's all the rage.

202. The wife went nuts when someone posted an empty sleeve through the letterbox. I said I couldn't see any arm in it...

203. It was cracking the flags the day the plastic surgeon moved in next door. Fifteen minutes later, he'd melted...

204. This dog asked me to tell it a joke. So I said: Knock, knock. And the dog flew at the door, going: Woof, woof, woof, woof, woof!!!

205. I said, I was driving home last night, when the missus rang and told me how much she loved me. She said, aww, I bet you filled up, didn't you? I said, did I heckers like: I'd still a hundred miles left in the tank!

206. I took my car for a mini-valet. Bloke said, tenner please, mate. I said, a tenner? Mini-valets a fiver it says over there! He said, it's not a Mini you're driving though, is it? It's an Insignia!

207. Author: I'm writing this sweeping epic about a battalion of British soldiers, charging across no-man's-land with fixed bayonets to capture miles of enemy trenches. Agent: Sounds a bit over the top to me.

208. There was this shoplifter on his way out of the book shop, cussing and swearing with an Oxford English Dictionary under his arm. Whey hey, I thought: he's got away with words...

209. Having a spot of bother with the Christmas tree lights, I asked the wife to check whether they were working or not. She said, yes, they are...no, they're not...yes, they are...no, they're not...yes, they are...

210. I rue the day I became addicted to helter-skelters: I've been on a downward spiral ever since.

211. A large sink hole has appeared in the fast lane of the M25: the police are looking into it.

212. It wasn't easy writing a novel without punctuation. Seriously, I had to pull out all the stops...

213. I went to a cannibal's birthday party. We started off with a finger buffet.

214. Me and the bloke who invented reclining chairs: we don't half go back a long way.

215. I watched this documentary about 12th Century nun's clothing, then straight after a film starring Bruce Willis, battling money-grabbing terrorists in an LA skyscraper. Old Habits Die Hard.

216. Did you hear about the cowardly cavalry officer that was court-martialled? He was released without charge.

217. I had to take the wife to hospital after she fell downstairs and broke her ankle. On the plus side, I've finally discovered where I left my roller skates.

218. So I said, who had a number one hit with Tiger Feet? Mud! came the reply. I said, that's right, that's right, that's right, that's right!

219. I've just been held up at gunpoint by this broad-billed-bird, dressed as a highwayman. Someone said it was Duck Turpin.

220. Pet food giant, Spillers, have pulled out of a deal to sponsor the England football team. It was thought they'd look a bit stupid with WINALOT on their shirts.

221. I was distraught when I forgot to record Coronation Street for the wife. Don't worry about it, she said, it's no drama...

222. A starving cannibal said he was going to eat my ticker. I thought, he's a man after my own heart.

223. I was offered a job cleaning mirrors. Sounds good, I thought: I can see myself doing that...

224. Our kid went to court, accused of strangling a smurf, but was acquitted on a technicality. Honestly, he'd get away with blue murder.

225. I was at the footie, eyeing up this bloke in the dugout with a blue smock on, clinging to a brush, mop and bucket. Apparently it was the caretaker manager.

226. All I got for Christmas was a bag of boiled sweets. So I went straight to the pub to drown my sorrows. Bar, humbug.

227. I've just seen a snake run over by a motorbike. If you don't believe me, here's a picture: $

228. What's the difference between a village and a hamlet? One's a small, rural settlement and the other's a big, fat cigar.

229. I said to the missus, nip down the shops and fetch corned beef, potatoes, leeks, carrots and onions...and don't make a hash of it!

230. I phoned this Chinese dentist. I said, can I book an appointment this afternoon? About tooth hurtee...?

231. A former chef made his debut for United and won a dubious last minute penalty to win the game. By all accounts, he made a right meal of it...

232. I was walking past the church when this bloke fell out of the bell tower. I thought it was the vicar at first. Then I realised: it was just a dead ringer!

233. Did you know that the seasons are all named after coils of turned metal? Except for winter and summer, of course; oh, and autumn...

234. This bloke asked me what I knew about Sherlock Holmes. I said, do you mean that block of flats opposite the park?

235. Window fitter goes to the doctors, demanding something for the pain. Quack says, how about a lump of putty?

236. I asked the woman next door what her supermarket habits were. She said, Lidl and often...

237. Two blokes on the big dipper. One says, if it turns upside down, do you think we'll fall out? Other says, don't be daft: we've been best pals for more than forty years!

238. I told my policewoman girlfriend there was no spark between us anymore. So she tasered me...

239. She said, there's a parcel van just pulled up outside, dearest. He said, is it TNT, darling? She said, I'm not sure, dearest; but judging by the shape of the package, it might be a few sticks of dynamite!

240. I applied for a loan to open a jigsaw factory but the bank turned me down flat. I've been in pieces ever since.

241. Attendance was excellent for the AGM of the projectile vomiting society. In actual fact, it was heaving...

242. I went to a Scottish pyromaniac's housewarming party. The theme was Burns Night.

243. What would you get if you crossed the North Atlantic with the Titanic? About half way!

244. I joined the local thesaurus club. Rule number one was: no gabbing, yapping, chattering, gossiping, nattering, chit-chatting or heart-to-hearts while someone is talking.

245. Two packets of crisps on a bench in the pouring rain, when a taxi pulls up. Driver says, do you want a lift? Crisp says, no, thanks: we're Walkers...

246. I was rudely awoken last night to find this bloke, making off with my garden gates. I didn't say anything to him, like; he might have taken a fence.

247. My application to join the Tourette's society has been accepted. I'm being sworn in next Friday.

248. Now Christmas is over, I'm having a dry month: dry Martini, dry white wine, dry sweet cider...

249. Apparently my long lost auntie has left me a priceless watch in her will. I'm just praying it's not a wind up.

250. Southerners have been advised to stay indoors as strong winds and blizzards continue to batter the UK. Northerners will need their big coats on.

251. I've just resigned from my gritter-driver's job at Humberside county council. They've asked me to reconsider, but I've told them no chance: Hull can freeze over first.

252. It's just been on the telly that, when things warm up, they expand. That's it, then: I'm not fat, after all...I'm hot!

253. Struggling with the morning crossword, I googled 16 across: missing Medieval servant. It came up Page not found.

254. I used to be a postman in China, but got fed up of rowing out to sea to deliver all the junk mail.

255. Two fish in a tank. One says, you drive: I'll man the guns.

256. Driving past this army camp, I noticed all the soldiers were fainting and falling over. Ooh look, I thought: a passing out parade...

257. So I said, I got that street cleaner's job, darling. She said, marvellous news, dearest. Will you have to go on any training courses? I said, apparently not, darling: the boss says I can just pick it up as I go along.

258. I was involved in a prang with an Elvis impersonator. I was alright, like, but he was all shook up...

259. Did you hear about the former drugs dealer that had his bike stolen? After weeks of anguish, he's finally back pedalling.

260. I ran cross-legged into Poundland. I said, do you have anywhere I can spend a penny...?

261. This bloke offered to sell me a bed for a tenner. I told him I was definitely interested; but I'd prefer to sleep on it first.

262. I was on the way out of the post office when the manager stopped me and accused me of stealing a book of stamps. I said, take that back, matey, or I'll stick one on you!

263. Our kid turned up with an ill-looking sea creature; eight arms and a long, thin body, smothered in tentacles. There you go, bro, he said, there's that sick squid I owe you.

264. So I said, I drove through a big puddle outside the hospital, soaking a long line of doctors, waiting at the bus stop. He said, any wet nurses? I said, no, thank goodness: there was only me saw it happen...

265. The tax evader's cricket club were 752-2 at close of play. Asked if he was going to declare, the captain said, what do you think...?

266. I had the police round last night, complaining my dog was chasing this bloke on a bike. I said, it couldn't have been mine: it hasn't even got a bike...

267. Shepherd goes to the surgery. He says, doctor, doctor, I can't get to sleep at night. Quack says, have you tried counting sheep? Shepherd says, give it a rest, can't you?

268. Perish the thought; but, if anyone ever aims a gun at the US President, you'll hear scores of secret service agents shouting, Donald duck!

269. I've bought a house on Mount Kilimanjaro. Yup, I'm off to foreign climbs.

270. They say 40 is the new 30: try telling that to a flipping speed camera, I thought!

271. I'm not impressed with these new energy saving lightbulbs. I've still got to get up to switch them on.

272. 1st villain: I broke into this shop last night and got away with loads of pictures of houses, all worth hundreds of thousands of pounds! 2nd villain: You daft sod: you know you've robbed the flipping estate agents, don't you?

273. So I said, did you do your chores? He said, chores; what chores? I said, I'll have a double whisky and lemonade, thank you very much...

274. I've lost my bank book. If anyone finds it, I strongly recommend the chapter on Barclays.

275. There's this bloke down the pub that's started work for a blue chip company. Good luck to him, I say: I prefer mine golden brown with lashings of salt and vinegar.

276. I was out raking the lawn when Mick Jagger walked past. I said, fancy giving us a hand, Mick? He said, haven't you heard, mister? A Rolling Stone gathers no moss.

277. This bloke went for an X-ray and was told he had a hole in his heart. It wasn't until he got home he realised he had a polo in his top pocket.

278. I used to go out with a girl with a double-barrelled surname. She was a good old stick Alison Twelve-Bore.

279. There was this bloke coming out of the church, covered in spaghetti and tomato sauce. I think it must have been the local pasta.

280. I'm worried the wife might be money laundering. She's just washed my jeans with £25 in the back pocket.

281. Did you hear about the doctor that only gave his patient two years? The patient blew his head off with a shotgun and now the judge's given him forty!

282. I accidentally set fire to my anorak...now it's a blazer!

283. Her: I've found a pen: it's not yours, is it? Him: I don't think so. Let's have a look and I'll soon tell you. Hang on a minute, it must be...it's my handwriting!

284. I went on The Apprentice and Lord Sugar sent me to the stores for a left-handed screwdriver and a long stand. I came back three hours later with a tin of Tartan paint.

285. This plank of mahogany said, so, you wanna piece of me? It was hard wood.

286. Newsflash: nearly £1000 of merchandise was stolen from the local cinema this afternoon. Police are on the look-out for anyone carrying two hot dogs, a medium bucket of popcorn and a small diet coke.

287. First day in the factory, the missus got a right old roasting off one of the gaffers. I said, big wig, like? She said, no, but he had one heck of a comb-over...

288. I took my bath back to the showroom when it kept leaking water. Assistant said, it's because there's no plug in it. I said, no plug? You never told me it was electric!

289. Did you hear about the faddy cannibal who turned his nose up at a portion of poached oil tycoon? He said it was a bit rich for him.

290. I said, doctor, doctor, I keep thinking I'm a ghost. He said, get a life, man...

291. My job in the sellotape factory: I've told them where to stick it.

292. I wasn't sure about my hair transplant at first; but I can't deny it's starting to grow on me...

293. There was this young couple in the supermarket, dressed as barcodes. I said, are you two by any chance an item...?

294. I went to the doctors to discuss my infatuation with Sigourney Weaver, Jennifer Lawrence and Angelina Jolie. Quack said, it's not good news, I'm afraid...you've got a heroine addiction!

295. This bloke tried selling me a blunt pencil. I told him thanks for the offer; but there wasn't really much point, was there?

296. Two piles of vomit, walking along the high street. One says, we're lost, aren't we? Other says, are we heckers like: I was brought up round here.

297. Did you hear about the cannibal who was dismissed from the army on account of his breakfast habits? Whenever boiled eggs were on the menu, he insisted upon having soldiers with them.

298. I hit this bloke over the head with a scrapbook. He told me to cut it out.

299. What time does Andy Murray go to bed? Tennish.

300. I went to the chippie and asked for fish and chips twice. Fryer said, alright, alright: I heard you the first time!

Bad Dad Jokes: 301-450 – Worse Still!!!!

301. My new job, hand-painting the Humber Bridge: I've only been there a week and it's already starting to take its toll.

302. I called the police after a lorry shed a load of cutlery near our house. Asked where exactly, I said, turn left at the fork in the road...

303. I've just bought my first house for £350. Alright, so it was during a game of Monopoly; but it's a start, isn't it…?

304. The park flasher has dismissed all talk of retirement. He says he's going to stick it out for at least another couple of years.

305. I bought a chocolate fireguard but wish I hadn't bothered. It was about as much use as a chocolate fireguard.

306. It's just been on the news that the local sewage works is facing closure. Apparently ten million jobbies are at risk.

307. A widescreen plasma was chasing this bloke down the street and gaining fast. Ooh look, I thought: catch-up TV.

308. I wasn't impressed with the pirate DVD I bought. When I put it on, there wasn't a pirate in sight: it was a blooming cowboy film!

309. Why do burglars stay in bed all day? Because they need their booty sleep.

310. I got a wok for my birthday even though I despise Chinese food. No worries, though; I've put that much weight on of late, I can always use it to iron my shirts in.

311. I went to A&E after picking up the iron up instead of the phone. Nurse said, that explains one burned ear: what happened to the other? I said, it rang again five minutes later.

312. Today's conundrum: why did Kamikaze pilots wear helmets?

313. I start my new postman's job tomorrow. It's not quite what I was looking for; but at least I'm not walking the streets...

314. Two pals, touring Scotland. One says, there's still no sign of the Forth Road Bridge. Other says, I'm not surprised. We haven't been over the other three yet.

315. I went swimming with sharks but wish I hadn't bothered. It cost me an arm and a blinking leg...

316. There's this 1980s pop quiz doing the rounds online. I've only been on three times and I'm already on Level 42.

317. I want to state here and now that I *don't* have an obsession with tidiness...I just wanted me to clear that up.

318. My cross-eyed girlfriend: I'm sure she's seeing someone else.

319. I bought the wife this winter garment twenty years ago and I'm proud to say it still fits her today. Everyone agrees: it's the best scarf she's ever had...

320. It's just been on the news that the police are looking for a mass murderer with one eye. If he was a dangerous as they're making out, wouldn't you think they'd be using both eyes...?

321. I was offered a job in a circus, training frogs. I said, but I don't know the first thing about frogs. Gaffer said, don't worry about it; you can just make it hop as you go along...

322. My sister has finished with her painter and decorator boyfriend. She was sick of him telling her she needed two coats on.

323. It didn't half cheer me up when I read that 60% of the human body is water. It means I'm not fat, after all...I'm just flooded.

324. Did you hear about the bloke that fell ill after eating a box of Christmas decorations? He came down with tinselitis.

325. I called round to see an old flame. Her mother said she'd just gone out...

326. The wife wasn't impressed when I suggested calling the new cat Fyffe. In actual fact, she went blooming bananas!

327. I went down the pub and got poked in the eye by an antler. Flipping stag party!

328. Someone said there was a decent turn on at the working men's club. When I got there, it was an Arctic sea bird with a big, yellow beak.

329. Apparently there's a part-job going at the fruit n veg shop. Twenty hour per week: celery negotiable.

330. I submitted a passport application form. I got it in a headlock and it tapped out.

331. Him: That black and white mongrel near us: I think it might be homeless. Her: What makes you say that? Him: Because it's sleeping woof...

332. Did you hear about the woman who was rushed to hospital after mistaking a daffodil bulb for an onion? Doctors have said she won't be out until the spring.

333. I'm writing a screenplay about female menstruation in the 19th Century. It's a period drama.

334. I never realised Attila the Hun and Conan the Barbarian had the same middle name. The.

335. Last night's documentary about the Boston Strangler. Gripping.

336. The bloke who invented pass the parcel...you've got to hand it to him.

337. I went on holiday and got hit by a tidal wave of tonic water. I was almost Schwepped away.

338. The missus reckons I've two big faults: number one I don't listen and some other nonsense she was rattling on about...

339. Our kid's going out with a girl from the jam factory. I spotted them in the pub last night, having a couple of jars...

340. I told the doctor I couldn't sleep at night. He said, try kipping on the edge of the bed...you'll soon drop off.

341. The woman next door may be nine months pregnant, but she's still insisting upon her daily trip to the retail park. Talk about shop until she drops...

342. I took my iPhone back to the shop when it started leaking water. I said, I think it might have been tapped.

343. This bloke asked if I'd give him a hand back to his car with a bottle of water. No wonder: it wasn't half an Evian.

344. I've received an anonymous delivery of almonds, three weeks in a row. Whoever is behind it is sending me nuts.

345. The old girl down the street has been found dead in her washing machine. Such a shame; but at least she died in Comfort.

346. I arrived home in a state of shock after a speeding laundry van lost control and spilled a load of dirty underwear across my bonnet. The wife said, goodness me; was there any skid marks? I said, any skid marks? I was nearly blooming sick, that's all!

347. This bloke asked me if I fancied a sparring session with Mike Tyson. I said, you can count me out...

348. I told the quack I couldn't stop thinking I was a bottle of German gin. He said, Schnapp out of it, man!

349. Apparently there's an armed siege taking place at the ice-cream parlour. Police have coned off the area.

350. I had a bad accident at the saw mill. My other half reckons we should sue for compensation.

351. It was only after reading his name backwards that I realised President Mugabee came from Yorkshire.

352. I nipped to the shop for a couple of sheets of fine sandpaper, but all they had was multi-packs. Ah well, I thought: sometimes you have to take the rough with the smooth.

353. Ok, so I enjoy the occasional tipple of brake fluid? People say I'm addicted, but I'll have you know I can stop whenever I want...

354. I start my new job at the deodorant factory on Monday...roll on.

355. It's just been on the news that a local undertaker has patented a glass coffin. He reckons it's bound to catch on, but I'm not so sure...remains to be seen.

356. My bid for a job lot of Australian toilet seats has been accepted. Yup, it's a dunny deal.

357. I went to the casino and spent £5000 on chips. The chef didn't clock out until 6 o'clock in the morning.

358. So I said, these new trousers: there's holes in both pockets. She said, why did you buy them, then? You must be losing it. I said, losing it? I'm down to my last fifty pence, that's all!

359. I smothered myself in strawberry preserve then went upstairs with my guitar. You can't beat a spot of jamming.

360. This label on my new trousers said, 32 leg. I thought, crikey, that would fit four octopuses.

361. I decided to have a conversation with the missus when the Wi-Fi went down. I couldn't believe it when she told me she didn't work at Woolworth's anymore...

362. This woman asked me if I knew where the remote control factory was. I said, have you tried the Channel Islands?

363. The bloke who invented TV remote controls has died. He was found two weeks later down the back of the settee.

364. My staircase has just been decorated. Yup, it won a Victoria Cross for single-handedly storming an enemy machine-gun post.

365. I used to be addicted to bath nights. But I'm glad to say I've been dry for five years now.

366. Our kid's suing the local bakery for using his signature to mark its hot cross buns...X

367. I was going to invest in a Chinese distillery but decided against it. Whisky business.

368. Bloke trying on shoes. He says, they still feel a bit tight. Assistant says, try them with the tongue out. He says, I'm athraid th'till a bit on th'the th'tight th'side...

369. My guided tour of the convent. It was a bit of a nun event...

370. That book I was writing about the perils of excessive sunbathing: I've decided to stick it on the back burner.

371. I turned down a free ticket to go and see Cats in London. If it'd been a musical or something, I might have considered it...

372. Travel news: local roads remain paralysed after an accident involving a lorry load of pulverised tobacco. A police spokesman said it was his sad duty to announce that the driver had snuffed it.

373. What were General Custer's final words? Look at all them flipping Indians!

374. I put the telly on and guess what? It didn't fit!

375. Bloke goes into a pub with a pair of jump leads tied round his neck. Landlord says, you're not going to start anything, are you...?

376. I bought a Blur alarm clock. Every morning, I rise to the sound of Parklife; except on Wednesday, when I get rudely awoken by the dustmen...

377. I nearly lost my dog in the blacksmiths: it made a bolt for the door.

378. Historians have discovered the headstone of the world's oldest man on the M1 near Sheffield. Apparently was 162 and his name was Miles from London.

379. I got into an argument with a pest controller. He should have kept his trap shut.

380. The wife was doing the crossword. She said, sixteen across: famous ruler? I said, it's not the Helix 30 cm shatterproof, is it?

381. Apparently there's a lunatic going round, terrorising people with burning matches. Police fear it's only a matter of time before he strikes again.

382. I put Zulu on but wish I hadn't bothered. It was all about a toilet attendant at Chester Zoo!

383. Woman goes in the lingerie shop and asks if they have any satin knickers. Assistant says, sorry, madam: we don't stock anything pre-worn...

384. Our match against the yoghurt factory X1 didn't exactly go as planned. We got absolutely mullered.

385. This bloke asked me what I knew about swordplay. I said, give me five minutes and I'll run you through.

386. It's just been on the news that a highly dangerous, psychic dwarf has escaped from prison. Yup, a small medium is at large...

387. The bloke who invented bridges: you wouldn't want to cross him.

388. I sent off for the boxset of hit TV series, Lost. It arrived on time, like; but now I can't find it...

389. So I said, what a day: I nearly got eaten alive by a starving cannibal. He said, blimey; I'll bet your heart was in your mouth, wasn't it? I said, in his more like!

390. The villain who broke into the knicker elastic factory: apparently he's looking at a five-year stretch.

391. After a long courtship, the bloke next door's announced his engagement to the girl from the string factory. Yup, they're finally tying the knot.

392. I moved to this street where all the kids have head lice but their parents are too miserly to spend anything on treatment. Talk about a tight-nit community.

393. My little brother, Sid, lost his ID last night. So now we just call him S...

394. This time tomorrow I'll be on the plane. Yup, I'm taking an inch off the bottom of the door.

395. I had this bloke round the house last night, flogging key rings. I soon fobbed him off.

396. Did you hear about the cannibal that was sacked from the building site? While everyone else was having brekkie, he was having a brickie...

397. This bloke bet me a tenner he could eat a pound coin. I said, go on, then: put your money where your mouth is.

398. If anyone missed last night's documentary about life in a red sauce factory, it's still available on Ketchup TV.

399. The wife sent me out for six cans of Sprite...but I picked 7 Up by mistake.

400. ET's been caught shoplifting. I always said he was light fingered.

401. This bloke asked me for my religious views. I said, if I stand on a chair in the back bedroom, I can just about make out St Mary's church steeple...

402. I'm tempted to tell the world about my new hair transplant; but I think I'll keep it under my hat for now.

403. The quack said I should have booked an appointment weeks ago when I told him I couldn't stop thinking everyone was a cat. I said, I know that, like; it's just that, well...I didn't want to put you out.

404. I passed 23 signs in a row, all saying: Reduce Speed Now. Well, it must have worked; because, when I went in HMV, I spotted the Keanu Reeves film of the same title in the bargain bucket, priced just £1.99.

405. Did you hear about the former skin surgeon who was sacked on the first day of his new job on the building site? All he did was sit on his backside for the entire shift; this after telling everyone during his interview he was a brilliant grafter...

406. I've still no idea where I put the colander. Honestly, I've got a mind like a blooming sieve.

407. Window shopping with the wife, I pointed out this diamond encrusted Rolex. I said, that's the one I'd get. Next thing, Cyclops had me pinned against a wall. He said, you wanna piece of me...?

408. I arrived to home to find the missus with a pad on her knee, making a sketch of the window. Whey hey, I thought: she's drawing the curtains!

409. Our kid's still only on chapter 2 of the book he's writing about revolutionary nose picking techniques. I've told him it's about time he got his finger out.

410. I once spent three years living in a cellar. I was in a bit of a dark place at the time.

411. Why did the bubble gum cross the road? Because it was stuck to the chicken's foot.

412. I've been offered a job as a signpost erector...way to go!

413. This bloke asked me how many Motown groups I could name. I said, two or three...Four Tops.

414. This barber charged me twenty quid for a nostril hair trim. Talk about paying through the nose...

415. Student: I spent the summer holidays shoving bangers up pigeon's backsides, miss. Teacher: Backsides? Don't you mean rectum? Student: Wrecked 'em? It blew their blinking heads off!

416. I went to the dentist for three canines removing. I went home with a Cocker Spaniel, a Dalmatian and a flea bitten Heinz 57...

417. This bloke kept nagging me to help him put some air in his tyres. I told him to stop pressurising me.

418. I burst into tears when I finally finished the decorating. Yup, I came over all emulsional.

419. I asked this accident investigator if he'd much on today. He said, blooming shed loads...

420. Teacher: Can anyone tell me what a Fjord is? Pupil: Is it a Norwegian motor car, miss?

421. I went for this carpenter's job. When I got home, the wife said, well, did you get it? I said, get it? I absolutely nailed it!

422. Hubby: I've spent all afternoon sunbathing in the garden, darling, listening my Diana Ross CDs. Wifey: Three Degrees, dearest? Hubby: And the rest: it was cracking the flaming flags out there!

423. Bert tripped and fell over at the football match. Someone said, he's hurt his neck; quick, support his head! And the crowd began to sing, Bert 's head, clap-clap-clap, Bert's head, clap-clap-clap...

424. I bought a chocolate teapot but wish I'd not bothered. It was about as much use as a chocolate teapot.

425. For the first time in my life, I'm lost for words...flipping burglars nicked my Scrabble!

426. My computer may have beaten me during a game of chess; but it was no competition when it came to a bout of kickboxing, I can tell you...

427. Newsflash: Thieves broke into United's ground last night and emptied the contents of the trophy room. Police are looking for someone with a rolled up red and white carpet.

428. Did you hear about the dyslexic Yorkshireman that insisted upon walking about with a cat flap on his head?

429. The missus told me a cracking joke about a travelling iron. She creases me up, she really does...

430. I took my faulty PC back to the shop. Assistant said, hard drive, like? I said, not really; I only live round the corner.

431. The woman next door is back with her painter and decorator boyfriend; this after falling out with him over his obsession with rubber ducks. I can't see it lasting, mind; if you ask me, they're simply papering over the quacks...

432. Sixteen years ago this week, I had my front door stolen. I never found out who nicked it and I've never bothered replacing it, either. Sometimes, I don't think I'll ever get closure...

433. Patient: Doctor, Doctor, I keep thinking I'm a dog. Quack: I'll not tell you again: get off that couch!

434. I've started manufacturing catamarans in the attic. Sails are going through the roof.

435. I said, I've just been offered a job with the Chippendales. She said, get away; what doing, like? I said, you'll have to wait and see, won't you? All will be revealed...

436. This bloke offered me the complete works of Peter the Rabbit to alter his trousers for him. I thought, now there's a turn up for the books...

437. I'm stopping in all weekend, revising for my pest controller's exam. Yup, I'll be in the house...swatting.

438. I squeezed a spot and this puss popped out. Anybody want to buy a kitten?

439. Apparently the bloke who stole my diary has died. My thoughts are with him...

440. I've just won the most secretive person award for the third year in a row. I can't tell you how much it means to me.

441. The woman next door begged me not to tell anyone she was expecting. Don't you worry, I said: Mum's the word...

442. I saw a bottle of perming lotion having a fight with a pair of curling tongs. I think they must have been having a straightener.

443. The missus bought me a pair of baggy trousers and a ticket on a night boat to Cairo. I thought, this is madness...

444. I got into an argument with Mo Farah. He said, do you know I'm a quadruple Olympic champion at five and ten thousand metres? I said, alright, alright: there's no need to play the race card...

445. This bloke got out of a car and asked me the way to Liverpool. I said, leave your keys in the ignition, jump in the boot and you'll be there in ten minutes.

446. If there was a granny, a goat and an au pair, running the country, would we be living in a Nanny State...?

447. I said, blimey; it's blowing a blooming gale out there. She said, tell me about it. Anyone who ventures out in that lot...hats off to them!

448. Teacher: Can anyone define the word, metaphor? Pupil: Is it when two people bump into each other more than once, miss...?

449. I didn't get very far in last night's pop quiz. Question 2 was: who invented dandelion and burdock...?

450. Bloke goes to the bookies and asks for odds on a dragon flying over United's ground, first match of the season. Assistant says, sorry, sir, but dragons are mythical creatures, so it's impossible to process your request. Bloke says, alright, what's the odds on City gaining automatic promotion? Assistant says, and what colour dragon would that be, sir...?

Bad Dad Jokes: 451-601 – Unbearable!!!!

451. I was in the middle of a slap up meal when my phone rang. I said, I'll have to call you back later: I've a lot on my plate at the moment.

452. The bloke who delivers washing machines for Argos died yesterday. His funeral is next Wednesday, anytime between 9 and 4.

453. I sat on a hair dryer. It didn't half put the wind up me...

454. Teacher: Does anyone know what a 4X4 is? Pupil: Is it someone who's got four kids by four different fathers, miss?

455. All the wife could do was grunt and moan when I asked if she wanted me to pick fish and chips up on the way home. She said it was the worst mistake of her life, letting me name the twins...

456. I wasn't impressed when this waiter clouted me round the back of the head. It's the last time you'll get me out for a slap up meal, I can tell you.

457. My job at the nail factory: for those who haven't heard, I've knocked it on the head...

458. I spotted this chimney sweep, coming out of a nightclub at six in the morning? Dirty stop out.

459. For anyone who enjoys a good read, I can heartily recommend: How to Get Rich Quick by Robin Banks.

460. I've just been fired from the calendar factory. All I did was take a day off...

461. Hubby in the shower: Is there any shampoo, darling? Wifey: On the shelf, dearest. Hubby: But that's for dry hair, darling: mine's wet through...

462. I went to court, charged with murdering my next door neighbour with a sanding block. I wouldn't mind, like, but I only meant to rough him up a bit.

463. I arrived home after failing my driving test. She said, what did they pull you up on? I said, this long rope: the car was at the bottom of the river...

464. That bloke from the itching powder factory is one heck of a golfer. He only plays off flipping scratch!

465. Patient: Doctor, Doctor, I keep thinking I'm swimming in a big Parisian river. Quack: You're in Seine!

466. Him: I swatted three flies earlier: two males and a female. Her: How could you tell which was which? Him: The males were on a beer can and the female was on the phone.

467. This butcher rang. He said, I hear you've got a complaint about my meat? I said, can you repeat that? I have to say the loins not fantastic...

468. Lollipop ladies. They don't half make me cross.

469. So I said, why do you keep an empty milk bottle in the fridge? He said, it's just in case anyone fancies a black coffee...

470. I went to this birthday party, where all we did all day was sit in a big circle, passing round this clergyman, wrapped up in sheets of newspaper. It's the last time you'll catch me getting involved a game of pastor parcel, I can tell you.

471. I said, I'm thinking of taking the wife to Italy for the week. He said, Genoa? I said, I should hope so: we've been married twenty-five years.

472. A mate of mine put his Cool for Cats album on EBay. I said, what's up, like; are you feeling the Squeeze?

473. After years of torment, I'm finally convinced the wife is seeing someone else. We moved to John O'Groats and still have the same window cleaner.

474. I asked this bloke how his holiday to Cleethorpes went. He said, don't even go there...

475. 27 years after starting work at the bread shop, the wife's suddenly decided she hates it. I reckon she's going through some kind of mid-loaf crisis.

476. I've just been offered a job as Prince Harry's chauffeur. Honestly, I'm not taking you for a ride...

477. Couple delayed at the airport. She says, apparently it's an air traffic controller strike. He says, Herr Traffic Controller? I should have known it would be something to do with the blooming Germans!

478. I was sure I could hear onions, singing Bee Gees songs in the fridge; but when I checked, it was just the chives talking...

479. Bloke goes to the doctors, thinking he's a paper bag. He says, and another thing: everyone I come into contact with suddenly comes down with a bad dose of flu. Quack says, so, you're not a paper bag, after all...you're a carrier!

480. This bloke asked me one, two, three questions in a row about Meatloaf. I got the first and last ones right but the second one wrong. Ah, well, I thought: two out of three ain't bad...

481. Apparently people are saying there should be more diversity on TV. Give it a rest: that flipping annoying dance troupe has been on every week since they won Britain's Got Talent!

482. My obsession with Blondie lyrics: I'm determined to beat it...one way or another.

483. If you choked a Smurf, what colour would it turn...?

484. Our kid's checked his bank account and reckons he can live comfortably for the rest of his life...just so long as he pops his clogs a week on Sunday.

485. I had this bird impressionist round, saying I owed him a tenner. I told him to go and whistle for it!

486. Good King Wenceslas went into the pizza shop and ordered a meat feast. Assistant said, how would you like that done, mate? Deep and crisp, and even...?

487. There was this pregnant woman at the bus stop. I said, when's it due, like? She said, a week on Monday. I said, stuff that, I may as well walk...

488. Bloke goes to the quacks. He says, doctor, doctor, I keep thinking I'm a goat. Quack says, I hope you're not taking it out on the kids.

489. I knocked on this teacher's door. This voice said, he's busy marking exercise books: he' says he'll be out in a tick...

490. That invoice I received from the origami society: I'm not sure what to make of it...

491. I've applied for a town crier's job. Don't laugh; I reckon I might be in with a shout!

492. Our kid says he wants to be a Singer when he grows up. I keep telling him: there's not much of a living to be made as a sewing machine...

493. I was telling the missus how this bloke at work broke a leg skiing. She said, on the piste, like? I said, on the piste? By the sounds of it, he'd had a right old skinful!

494. Wifey: I've got a couple of birthday tips for you, dearest. Number one: forget the past, because you can never change it. Hubby: What's number two, darling? Wifey: Forget the present as well, because I didn't get you one!

495. This sign on the motorway said: Animals in Road. Yeah, right, I thought; next thing, there was this 60s pop group in the fast lane, performing House of the Rising Sun!

496. I arrived home with a privet under my arm. The missus said, what's this, like? I thought you'd gone to buy a telly? I said, don't blame me; it was you who said if to bring a Bush if there weren't any deals on Sony...

497. So I said, which way to the maternity suite, mate? This porter replied, third door on the left: the one that says push, push, push on it.

498. Our new GP is Count Dracula. Apparently every time his door opens, he says, necks please...

499. Apparently Santa's given up smoking. He said it was bad for his Elf.

500. Our kid's going out with a girl from the hot water bottle factory. I wasn't sure at first; but I can't deny I'm beginning to warm to her...

501. I went to the pet shop and bought ten bees in a jar. When I got home, though, there was eleven, so I rang the shop and explained. Owner said, don't worry about it: the last one's a free-bee.

502. It's been on the news that sales of houmous and taramasalata have fallen dramatically. Experts are blaming a double dip recession.

503. Boxer goes to the chippy. He says, fish and chips please, missus. Assistant says, any scraps? He says, what do you think...?

504. I've finally retired from my job, sprinkling little sparkly bits on Christmas cards. I think it's fair to say I had a glittering career.

505. Quasimodo goes in a pub and orders a whiskey. Barman says, which one: Glenfiddich, Grants or White Horse? Quasimodo says, the Bells, the Bells!

506. I asked this bloke what he thought of his new inflatable mattress. He said, if I'm entirely honest, it's been a bit of a let-down…

507. Apparently the footballer's Christmas nativity play had to be cancelled when the organisers couldn't find anyone to play the parts of the three wise men.

508. I auditioned for a part in a dog walking drama. Miracle upon miracle, I was offered the lead…

509. I'm thinking of going into business, ridding the streets of discarded chewing gum. I just need a bit of help getting it off the ground.

510. I went for this door-to-door salesman's job. I said, is it cold calling, like? He said, not this time of year…but you'll need your big coat on when winter gets here.

511. Expectant mother goes to the doctors, complaining about throwing up every time she goes to a funeral. Quack says, I wouldn't worry too much: it's probably just a bit of mourning sickness.

512. Bloke goes in a pub and asks how much the beer is. Barman says, three quid a pint or a fiver a pitcher. He says, just give us a pint...forget the photo!

513. This policeman asked me to identify myself. So I looked in the mirror and said: Yup, that's definitely me!

514. So I said, doctor, doctor, ever since I experienced that bad bout of flu, I've kept thinking I'm this small, Middle Eastern country. He said, try not to worry: it's probably just a bit of Qatar.

515. This surgeon removed my gall bladder then told me a joke. I think it's fair to say he had me in stitches...

516. It's my pickpocket friend's birthday tomorrow. As a special surprise, I've stuck a tenner in his Grandma's purse for him.

517. I met this bloke yesterday with a wooden leg called Stan. In case you're wondering, I never found out what his other leg was called...

518. Black bull goes in a boozer. Barman says, we nearly named our pub after you, mate. Black Bull says, what, Eric...?

519. I went to the doctors with a peanut in my ear. The quack poured some melted chocolate in and it came out a Treat.

520. The ventriloquist doll I fell in love with...apparently she's already spoken for.

521. A lorry spilled twenty pallets of smart TVs and laptop computers in the Toxteth area of Liverpool earlier. Police said the road was closed for nearly three minutes.

522. I bought the wife a fridge for her birthday. You should have seen her face light up when she opened it.

523. This note on my wage slip said: tear along dotted line. So I positioned myself at one end and ran as fast as I could to the far side...

524. Kid arrives home after a night out in his dad's Ferrari. He says, I'll give you the good news first: the air bags are brilliant!

525. I not saying the bloke next door is tight, but he's just had double glazing fitted so the kids can't hear the ice-cream van...

526. What do you call a German, strumming on an imaginary, six-string Hofner Bass? Herr Guitar.

527. If moths like the light so much, why do they come out at night...?

528. I was flabbergasted when I was accused of stealing a gobstopper from the local shop. Talk about hard to swallow...

529. He said, have I told you my wife is off to the Holy Land? I said, Mecca, like? He said, no, she's going on her own accord...

530. I went to the doctors, thinking I was a bucket. Quack said, I must admit, you are looking a bit pail...

531. Apparently 200 cans of Red Bull have been stolen from the local supermarket. Some people, honestly: I don't know how they can sleep at night.

532. So I said, I've just been attacked by a pushbike; third time this week. He said, vicious cycle, like? I said, too right it was!

533. I went for this interview and was asked where I saw myself two years from now? I said, and can you please explain where in the advert it says I have to have 2020 vision?

534. The doctor warned me to watch my drinking. So I'm off to find a boozer with a big mirror in it.

535. My first love was a one-armed potholer. Believe it or not, I still carry a torch for her twenty years later.

536. I said, what do you think to the idea of an EU migrants cap, then? He said, not much; if they want a new hat, they should be made to pay for it the same as everyone else.

537. I've offered the woman next door a fiver to let me have a go on her Stannah stair-lift. It looks like she's going to take me up on it.

538. After a recent spate of ladder thefts, a police spokesman declined to comment upon how investigations were going, other than to say that steps were being taken...

539. I phoned this waste disposal company. I said, is it alright if I have a skip outside my house? This voice said, have a game of hopscotch if you like, pal: I'm not stopping you!

540. There's a bloke at work who reckons his middle name is Melton Mowbray. If you ask me, he's telling pork pies.

541. What's green, got six legs and wears checked trousers? Rupert the Snooker Table.

542. My deep sea diving business has hit trouble. I'm struggling to keep my head above water...

543. I'm not sure I agree with this NHS blanket ban on patients smoking. What are they meant to do, like? Wear two pairs of pyjamas?

544. There was this bloke, peeling spuds in the back garden. Whey hey, I thought: he's vegging out!

545. This waiter fetched me a glass of smiling pop. I said, I never ordered this! He said, yes, you did: it's your happy Tizer!

546. I told the wife I was thinking of buying a pneumatic drill. She said, and can you please explain what's wrong with the old one...?

547. Ever wondered why money always goes to money? It's the law of have riches...

548. Our kid's going on a caveman's stag do. Apparently they're off clubbing.

549. Pope arrives in Liverpool and is immediately approached by a youth, asking if he can help with his hearing. Pope puts his hands on the youth's ears, whispers a prayer, then says, how's your hearing now? Youth says, I don't know...it's not till next Friday.

550. Apparently there was a shooting last night, involving a starting pistol. Police think it might be race related.

551. I entered further education and was dumped straight into a class of Hawaiian exchange students. Yup, I was in the aloha sixth...

552. Roofers: they've got a slate loose.

553. I phoned the incontinence hotline. This voice said, can you hold, please?

554. Our kid reckons he's opening a second-hand bookshop; but I wouldn't take it as read...

555. There was this soldier, pruning hedges and cutting the grass. I think he must have been home on gardening leave.

556. The missus wasn't happy when I booked her two days away, stacking shelves in a supermarket. I don't know why: it her who said she fancied a Spar weekend.

557. A pallet of inflatable mattresses went missing overnight. Word on the street is that the culprit's decided to lilo a bit.

558. Ok, so I don't know the meaning of the word apocalypse: it's not the end of the world, is it?

559. The wife is adamant she's calling our new baby Camay. Personally, I'm washing my hands of it...

560. I went nuts when the guillotine I'd ordered never turned up. That's me all over, I suppose: always losing my head...

561. This bloke asked me who had a hit with Singing in the Rain? I said, was it Wet Wet Wet?

562. I went to visit my mate in prison. I said, what's the first thing you'll do when you get out? He said, I'm not at liberty to say...

563. Did you hear about the chef whose sleeve went up in flames while cooking dinner at the policeman's ball? He was arrested for possession of a fire arm.

564. The wife's been elected vice-president of the ladies hide and seek club. It's nothing more than she deserves: after all, she was a found her member...

565. I fell asleep in the cafe and woke up with a teabag in my mouth. I said, nobody treats me like a mug...

566. Boxer goes to the doctors with a broken jaw. Quack says, I was gobsmacked when I heard you'd lost again. He said, you were gobsmacked? How do you think I felt?

567. I ordered a new bed but the shop delivered a trampoline by mistake. The wife hit the roof...

568. Apparently the bloke who delivers washing machines for Argos died yesterday. His funeral is next Wednesday, anytime between 9 and 5.

569. I went to the shop for some eggs. Assistant said, medium? I said, no, but my aunty Hilda used to fancy herself as a bit of a clairvoyant...

570. There was this bloke, walking down the road with a pair of Bakewell tarts on his feet. Talk about shoe pastry!

571. I phoned my mate, asking when I could visit his new house in Australia. He said, not yet...we're a bit upside down at the moment.

572. It's just been on the news that a trio of cliff walkers perished overnight. Imagine that, I thought: three people and all with the same name as well.

573. Did you hear about the bloke who was arrested on his way home with the beef for Sunday dinner? He was charged with being in possession of a joint.

574. I fell over on the way home. This bloke said, vertigo? I said, not really; I only live round the corner...

575. I told my mate I'd signed up for the town tug of war team in the hope it might help me find a girlfriend. He said, have you pulled yet? I said, what do you think...?

576. A mate of mine's joined the Royal Tank Regiment. He says it's alright, like; but not without its Challengers.

577. I asked this bloke if he knew what the capital of Ethiopia used to be. He said, Abyssinia? I said, not if I see you first, matey...

578. Our kid never gets the drinks in. The nearest he came was when he got a round of applause...

579. I couldn't stop laughing when I spotted this misspelled sign on the motorway, saying: Cueing Traffic. Lo and behold, a mile further on, there were two Vauxhall Insignias, having a game of snooker.

580. I went in this bookshop. I said, how much are rule books for that crazy Harry potter flying broomstick game? Assistant said, Quidditch? I said, a quid each? I'd have paid at least a fiver!

581. I phoned the police after arriving home to discover someone had broken in and scoffed the entire contents of the fridge. I said, I'd like to report an ate crime...

582. Two pigs in a trough. One goes: Oink, oink! Oink, oink! Other grunts: You swine: I was going to say that!

583. I arrived home, covered in tinsel and baubles. I said, sorry I'm late, darling; I stopped off for a quick trim...

584. My ex wants her Buddy Holly records back...that'll be the day!

585. That bloke from the tip my sister was seeing: I'm glad to say she's dumped him.

586. I've been offered a job as a hand grenade salesman. The wife's not sure, like; but I reckon it's worth giving it a blast...

587. This bloke asked me who invented Stephenson's Rocket? I said, was it Isambard Kingdom Brunel?

588. The new butcher's shop that's opened: I've got a steak in it...

589. I didn't get that job at the kid's playground. Swings and roundabouts, I suppose...

590. While the wife was cooking a full English breakfast, I was busy running a bath. She said, what are doing, like? I said, just what it says on the back of the mushrooms: please wash before using.

591. This bloke said, can I be frank? I said, Zappa, Lampard or Sinatra...?

592. Have I told you the one about the paper boy? He blew away.

593. After United's latest defeat, the chairman is blaming the coach. For the blooming life of me, I can't see what the team bus has got to do with anything.

594. The Irish are sending a rocket ship to the sun: they're going at night so it doesn't catch fire.

595. I went in HMV. I said, do you have anything by the Pretenders? Assistant said, Brass in Pocket? I said, course I have; I never go anywhere with less than twenty quid.

596. This bloke asked me what I thought about weighing scales. I said, I'm not sure where I stand on them to be fair...

597. Apparently the call centre XI football team are in trouble after being caught fielding a team of ringers.

598. I've just been diagnosed with Rowan Atkinson syndrome. I've been prescribed a course of anti-Mr-Bean tablets.

599. The U2 sat nav I bought is hopeless: the streets have no name and I still haven't found what I was looking for...

600. My first cage fight was a complete disaster. I was knocked out by a hamster in the first round.

601. As the plumber said to his wife when their divorce became final...it's over Flo!

*   *   *

It's over Flo! And so, unfortunately, is The Daddy, endless hours of fun, tormenting family and friends with a relentless broadside of terrible jokes and puns - as only a Dad can!

So, how about we make a date and reconvene further down the line for another bout of laugh out loud laughter with The Daddy's big brother – coming your way soon!

If you genuinely can't wait, then please consider the following joke book titles by the same author:

Titanic Book of One Liners

That's Terrible! A Cringeworthy Collection of 1001 Really Bad Jokes

That's Terrible2: A Cringeworthy Collection of 1001 ~~Really Bad~~ Even Worse Jokes

Football's Biggest Ever Joke Book

Thank you Page:

From...

To..

Message...

....

....

....

....

....

....

....

....

....

Printed in Great Britain
by Amazon